Te
on the

G000128835

ex libris

Candlestick Press

Published by:
Candlestick Press,
Diversity House, 72 Nottingham Road, Arnold, Nottingham UK NG5 6LF
www.candlestickpress.co.uk

Design and typesetting by Diversity Creative Marketing Solutions Ltd.,
www.diversity.agency

Printed by Ratcliff & Roper Print Group, Nottinghamshire, UK

Selection and Introduction © Sarah Jackson, 2017

Cover illustration © Katie Tooke, 2017

Candlestick Press monogram © Barbara Shaw, 2008

© Candlestick Press, 2017

Donation to Samaritans www.samaritans.org

ISBN 978 1 907598 45 6

Acknowledgements:

The poems in this pamphlet are reprinted from the following books, all by
permission of the publishers listed unless stated otherwise. Every effort has
been made to trace the copyright holders of the poems published in this
book. The editor and publisher apologise if any material has been included
without permission or without the appropriate acknowledgement, and
would be glad to be told of anyone who has not been consulted. Thanks are
due to all the copyright holders cited below for their kind permission:

Billy Collins, *Taking Off Emily Dickinson's Clothes: Selected Poems*
(Picador, 2000)

Imtiaz Dharker, *The terrorist at my table* (Bloodaxe Books, 2006)
www.bloodaxebooks.com

Elaine Feinstein, *The Clinic, Memory: New & Selected Poems*
(Carcanet, 2017)

Louise Glück, *Faithful and Virtuous Night* (Carcanet, 2014)

Robert Hass, *The Apple Trees at Olema: New & Selected Poems*
(Bloodaxe Books; Harper Collins, 2011) www.bloodaxebooks.com

W. N. Herbert, *Cabaret McGonagall* (Bloodaxe Books, 1996)
www.bloodaxebooks.com

Sarah Jackson, *Pelt* (Bloodaxe Books, 2012) www.bloodaxebooks.com

Deryn Rees-Jones, *The Memory Tray* (Seren, 1994)

Michael Symmons Roberts, *The Half-Healed* (Jonathan Cape, 2008)

Where poets are no longer living, their dates are given.

Introduction

Whether you're a phone-phobe or a smartphone addict, the invention of the telephone has changed the ways that we make contact. Perhaps because of this, the phone has been both celebrated and denounced by writers over the last century. Virginia Woolf (1923), for instance, notes that 'the telephone, which interrupts the most serious conversations ... has a romance of its own.' And in 'Personism: A Manifesto' (1961), Frank O'Hara recalls 'realizing that if I wanted to I could use the telephone instead of writing the poem'.

O'Hara is not alone: writers from Francis Ponge to Pinkie Gordon Lane have made a connection between poetry and calling. In fact, the primary challenge for this anthology was not finding ten poems on the telephone, but choosing which poems to leave out – and it's with regret that I've not been able to answer to O'Hara's own 'phone call to the beyond' (1956), among others.

Each poem that follows, however, reveals the internal contradictions of the telephone, confusing relations between near and far, between public and private, and between connections and crossed wires. Ranging from love on the line to a dialogue with the dead, each poem says something different about the art of listening and our desire to find a voice. And each poem taps into the ways that we talk to ourselves as well as to other people.

Far from putting us 'in touch', as the old AT&T slogan says, new telecommunication devices often prompt fears about the distances between us. But there may be something about the possibilities and impossibilities of connection worth cherishing here: as the following poems suggest, the telephone has an uncanny capacity to tap into the unconscious and to hook us up with faraway voices. So, as you read, let these ten poems ring in your ears and jangle your nerves, echoing deep in the 'ear of your heart'.

Sarah Jackson

Sonnet

A man talking to his ex-wife on the phone.
He has loved her voice and listens with attention
to every modulation of its tone. Knowing
it intimately. Not knowing what he wants
from the sound of it, from the tendered civility.
He studies, out the window, the seed shapes
of the broken pods of ornamental trees.
The kind that grow in everyone's garden, that no one
but horticulturists can name. Four arched chambers
of pale green, tiny vegetal proscenium arches,
a pair of black tapering seeds bedded in each chamber.
A wish geometry, miniature, Indian or Persian,
lovers or gods in their apartments. Outside, white,
patient animals, and tangled vines, and rain.

Robert Hass

The Breather

Just as in the horror movies
when someone discovers that the phone calls
are coming from inside the house

so, too, I realized
that our tender overlapping
has been taking place only inside me.

All that sweetness, the love and desire—
it's just been me dialing myself
then following the ringing to another room

to find no one on the line,
well, sometimes a little breathing
but more often than not, nothing.

To think that all this time—
which would include the boat rides,
the airport embraces, and all the drinks—

it's been only me and the two telephones,
the one on the wall in the kitchen
and the extension in the darkened guestroom upstairs.

Billy Collins

The Telephone, Failing Again

This public box is
the only light in the whole terrace:
a single bulb in the wet
hedge, with the wind rising.
And the harsh buzz in
my ear   carries me
over some border to where it seems
we could just
lose one another this way
like unpaired shoes in
some accident of disorder,
and I cannot even trust
you would notice the loss.
Where are you where
in what moon
house   do these dry
noises now release their dust?

Elaine Feinstein

Visitors from Abroad

1.

Sometime after I had entered
that time of life
people prefer to allude to in others
but not in themselves, in the middle of the night
the phone rang. It rang and rang
as though the world needed me,
though really it was the reverse.

I lay in bed, trying to analyze
the ring. It had
my mother's persistence and my father's
pained embarrassment.

When I picked it up, the line was dead.
Or was the phone working and the caller dead?
Or was it not the phone, but the door perhaps?

2.
My mother and father stood in the cold
on the front steps. My mother stared at me,
a daughter, a fellow female.
You never think of us, she said.

We read your books when they reach heaven.
Hardly a mention of us anymore, hardly a mention of your sister.
And they pointed to my dead sister, a complete stranger,
tightly wrapped in my mother's arms.

But for us, she said, you wouldn't exist.
And your sister—you have your sister's soul.
After which they vanished, like Mormon missionaries.

3.

The street was white again,
all the bushes covered with heavy snow
and the trees glittering, encased with ice.

I lay in the dark, waiting for the night to end.
It seemed the longest night I had ever known,
longer than the night I was born.

I write about you all the time, I said aloud.
Every time I say "I," it refers to you.

4.

Outside the street was silent.
The receiver lay on its side among the tangled sheets;
its peevish throbbing had ceased some hours before.

I left it as it was,
its long cord drifting under the furniture.

I watched the snow falling,
not so much obscuring things
as making them seem larger than they were.

Who would call in the middle of the night?
Trouble calls, despair calls.
Joy is sleeping like a baby.

Louise Glück

Answermachine

Eh amna here tae tak yir caa:
Eh'm mebbe aff at thi fitbaa,
Eh mebbe amna here at aa

but jist a figment o yir filo
conjerrt up wance oan a while-o.
Therr's mebbe tatties oan thi bile-o;

Eh'm mebbe haein a wee bit greet
owre an ingin or ma sweet-
hert: or Eh'm bleedan i thi street

wi ma heid kickd in fur bein sae deep.
Eh'm mebbe here but fast asleep:
sae laive a message at thi bleep.

W. N. Herbert

Last Words

I
You have a new message:

Kiss the kids goodbye from me,
keep well, keep strong, *you know*
I'm sure, but here's to say I love you.
I lay these voice-prints
like a set of tracks, to stop
you getting lost among the tall trees,
beneath the break-less canopy,
on the long slow walk you take
from here without me.

II
You have a new message:

I do not want to leave you this
magnetic print, this digit trace,
my coded and decoded voice.
I do not want to leave you.
If I had a choice, my last words
would be carried to your window
on three slips of sugar paper in
the beaks of birds of paradise.
The words would say,
I'm sure you know,
I love you.

III
You have a new message:

I throw my voice across the city,
but it meets such a cacophony
we overload the network.
Countless last words divert
onto backup spools and hard drives.

Systems analyst turns archaeologist:
his fingertips, as delicate as brushes,
sift through sediment of conferences,
helpline hints, arguments and cold calls,
searching for the ones that say
You know, I'm sure, I love you.

IV
You have a new message:

This is the voice you hear in dreams,
this is the tape you cannot
bear to play. This is the voice-mail
you keep in a sealed silk bag
in a tin box in the attic.
But the message is out – in
the sick-beds and the darkened rooms;
in the billowing curtains
and the hush so heavy
you can hear the pulse in your wrists.
The message is out, in the ether,
in the network of digits and wires.
I know, you're sure, I love you.

V
You have a new message:

Don't remember this, don't save
this message. Keep instead
the pictures of last Sunday
in the park when summer
leaves were turning, roller-bladers
hand-in-hand, our boys
throwing fists of cut grass at each other.
Think of the extravagance of green,
and think especially of the sky,
its blinding cloudlessness.
*You know, I'm sure, but here's
to say I love you.*

VI
You have a new message:

This is the still, small voice
you longed to hear among the ruins.
This is the voice you fished
with microphones on long lines,
lowered into cracks between
the rocks of this new mountain.
And your ears ache with the effort,
the sheer will to listen, to conjure
my words, your name on my lips,
out of nowhere. *Here's to say...*

VII
You have a new message:

When a city is wounded,
before it moans, before it kneels,
it draws a breath and keeps it,
as though all phones are on hold,
all radios detuned, cathedrals locked
and all parks vacant.
It becomes a windless forest.
But remember, silence is not absence.
Learn to weigh them,
one against the other.
Each room of our house contains
a different emptiness. Listen.
Then break it. Say the words
you know, I'm sure, I love you.

VIII
You have a new message:

Do not forget the beauty of aeroplanes,
those long, slow pulses from the sun
which passed above our garden as
we lay out in the heat. Do not forget

their gentle night-time growl,
and how we used to picture people in them
– sleeping, talking – just as we were,
how we used to guess the destinations.
Do not forget the grace of aeroplanes,
the majesty of skyscrapers.
You know, I'm sure...

IX
You have a new message:

Still, a year on, you rifle through
black boxes, mail-boxes, voice-boxes,
in search of my final words.
You hunt them in the white noise
between stations on the radio, the blank
face of a TV with the aerial pulled out.
You walk in crowds, wondering
if my words were passed to him,
or her, as messenger. If I'd had time
to leave you words, you know, I'm sure,
they would have been *I love you*

X
You have a new message:

Now, my voice stored on your mobile,
I can tell you fifty times a day
how much *I love you.* 'Tell the kids',
I say. I don't know if you still do.
Sometimes, when you're out of town,
on trains, or in the shadow of tall buildings
the network breaks. You hear vowels
splinter in my throat,
as if struck by a sudden despair.

XI
You have a new message:

Where did my last words go?
Out and out on radio waves
into the all-engulfing emptiness,
fading to a whisper as they cross
from sky, to space, to nothing.
Or in, and in, as litany repeated
in your heart until all tape is obsolete.
Each cadence, every tongue-tick,
every breath is perfect, as you say
my words: *You know, I'm sure...*

XII
You have a new message:

There is nothing new in this.
My voice has printed like a bruise,
like a kiss, like a kiss so strong
it leaves a bruise. *I love you.*
You know it, I'm sure.
Beyond the smoking ruins,
ash-strewn streets and empty rooms,
above and beyond is a network.
It is a matrix of souls,
as fragile as lace,
but endless and unbreakable.

To save the message, press...

Michael Symmons Roberts

Connections

Deer walk upon our mountains, and the quail
Whistle about us their spontaneous cries;
Sweet berries ripen in the wilderness.

Wallace Stevens

I've dialled wrong, but she will talk.
My voice is her event, hers mine.
Am I English? *Saesneg*, I explain.

Winter, she says. In the wilderness.
The snow has never been so thick,
Caking her lonely wooden house.
The gutters spill water
The colour of flour. There are
Everywhere fir trees everywhere.
Breath becomes ice. In the woods,
Alone, a gunshot makes you listen.
There is silence.

The comforting roar of the hoarse brown bear.

I have stars, I say, English stars, a Welsh mountain I can
Just remember – *mynydd* – a word I can't pronounce too well.

In this room
I have newspapers
Three days old. A vase of dying flowers. The radio.
I have the voices of the politicians. Books. An atlas
I can't find either of us on.

We see each other for one split second:
How her red lips, laughing, grow redder in the cold.
How my hair has lost its summer lights, and my fingers tap
Needing a cigarette.

We rub noses in the moment of goodbye
Wanting our mouths to speak us closer,
Closer closer closer than the telephone.

Deryn Rees-Jones

The Red Telephone
(after Gary Young)

The boy stands at the bottom of the stairs clutching an apricot in his right hand so tightly that the juice runs down between his fingers. In his left hand he holds a toy telephone. It is red plastic with a curly white cord. It rings when you pull it along the ground by its string.

The boy pretends to telephone his mother who is upstairs in the bathroom, changing her tights because she has a ladder in her heel. *Fall down*, he whispers. *Fall down*. And I swear to you, when her kneecaps crack the bathroom tiles, the small red telephone rings.

Sarah Jackson

Text

I am sending a message again.
Maybe you can't hear it
through all the noise of lights
and the dangerous way things move
in that other city
where I think you are,
if I have the dates right, though
of course I could be wrong.

If you expected the message,
you would stand like this,
with your eyes open and focussed
on the screen, your ears closed.

The city I am in has lost
its volume control.
Every person in the place
is tuned to maximum.

Can you see the text?
Just to ask if you are safe
and well?

A phone shrills, a clock explodes,
in the next room, a TV switches on.
Everywhere, the sound of sirens, drills.
Cars screech, horns blare.

Where
are you?
Why have you stopped singing?

Imtiaz Dharker

The Telephone

"When I was just as far as I could walk
From here to–day,
There was an hour
All still
When leaning with my head against a flower
I heard you talk.
Don't say I didn't, for I heard you say—
You spoke from that flower on the window sill—
Do you remember what it was you said?"

"First tell me what it was you thought you heard."

"Having found the flower and driven a bee away,
I leaned my head,
And holding by the stalk,
I listened and I thought I caught the word—
What was it? Did you call me by my name?
Or did you say—
Someone said 'Come'—I heard it as I bowed."

"I may have thought as much, but not aloud."

"Well, so I came."

Robert Frost (1874 – 1963)